Zurich Transit

THE
SEAGULL
LIBRARY OF
GERMAN
LITERATURE

MAX FRISCH

Zurich Transit

TRANSLATED BY BIRGIT SCHREYER DUARTE

LONDON NEW YORK CALCUTTA

This publication was supported by a grant from the Goethe-Intitut India

Seagull Books, 2021

Originally published as *Zürich-Transit—Skizze eines Films* by Max Frisch
© Suhrkamp Verlag, Frankfurt am Main, 1993

First published in English translation by Seagull Books, 2010
English translation © Birgit Schreyer Duarte, 2010

ISBN 978 0 8574 2 818 9

British Library Cataloguing-in-Publication Data
A catalogue record for this book is available from the British Library

Typeset by Seagull Books, Calcutta, India
Printed and bound by WordsWorth India, New Delhi, India

For Ernst Schröder

CONTENTS

PREFACE

Film versions of literary works, which are realized through language alone and which exist without the moving pictures on the screen, are common and rarely successful. I attempted to do the opposite—to write with the film in mind. This meant, however, that only what can be achieved through filmic tools should be taken over, and the text (which, by the way, was developed with the kind assistance of filmmakers) cannot and should not be considered more than a suggestion, a plan, a rough outline. Anything that can be communicated only through words and not through pictures would be worthless. For a writer (less so for a playwright than a novelist) this is unfamiliar territory; therefore, I had to choose a fairly simple story, one for a beginner in film, which is what I am, and what I will likely remain, since the production had to be cancelled twice in the fall of 1965 due to mishaps. What is before you now is thus not a novel but the sketch of a film.

M. F.
December 1965

Zurich Transit

The sound of a plane engine at night—a parked jet, its motor dying down. Then silence. The asphalt. A car key someone has lost. / The searchlight on the airport's control tower revolving in the dark. ZURICH AIRPORT. Engine sounds, again from afar. / The Porsche key on the asphalt glints in the beam of the tower's searchlight. A man's shoe beside the key. Silence. The shoe approaches the Porsche key, then pushes it back and forth twice. Soon after, a male hand picks up the key. / A bird's-eye view of the fairly empty parking lot at night. Underneath a streetlight is parked a white Porsche. Not far from it, the man who found the key. He looks around to see if anyone is watching. Then the man, who's not wearing a coat, walks about for a while, feigning a casual attitude. Then turns around and, suddenly, striding across to the white Porsche, unlocks the door and gets in. / The Porsche's dashboard. It is obvious the man is unfamiliar with the car. His hand holds the key and gropes for the ignition. The man is only shown in silhouette. A young man. Finally, the engine starts up. The man's foot on the accelerator, then revving in neutral. / A bird's-eye view as before. The white Porsche, its lights off, backs out of the parking lot in an uncertain semicircle, then pauses for a few seconds. Then its lights come on and, with a sudden leap, it disappears into the night. / The man's left hand on the steering wheel. It is obvious he is not in full control of the car. / The screech of the wheels as the car turns the corners. A country road, rows of trees rushing past, briefly caught in the glare of the headlights. A horn blares. The brakes scream. Then, as the screen goes dark, an explosion.

Silence. The title appears. ZURICH TRANSIT. Opening credits roll against the background of a night-time accident. The police, cordoning off the area. Helmets and boots. / A truck trailer, tipped over at the side. Flames of burning gas on the street. / Men's silhouettes. / The burning Porsche in the distance. / The flashing light of an ambulance. / A fire extinguisher being used. Flames that it is unable to quench. / Finally, two paramedics—they lean an empty stretcher on a pole. End of opening credits.

Close-up of the burning Porsche. It has turned turtle and is completely destroyed. We can hear the flames crackle as the wheels begin to burn. / The same image, now as a photograph in a newspaper. Silence. The headline reads: 'Another Death on the Street'. Beside it is another picture, a man in the prime of his life—a pipe in his mouth, he is smiling, a familiar face, likeable and full of confidence. The caption above it reads: 'THEO EHRISMANN, Dipl.-Ing. †' / Then, the hands holding the newspaper. Wristwatch. Cufflinks. / Then, the reader in full view—it is the man in the picture but without the pipe and the smile. Not shocked—baffled. He thinks, he looks up—no, he isn't dreaming. / He is aboard a plane, a Caravelle. / He looks once more at his picture in the newspaper. An average face, probably a hard-working man, the kind who makes his way

4

up in the world. An engine starts up. / The illuminated letters: 'Please fasten your seatbelts.' / Ehrismann sits alone by the window, still holding the newspaper. A stewardess comes through, wearing a fixed smile, checking to her left and right for fastened seatbelts. As she passes Ehrismann—

STEWARDESS (*in English*).
Can I help you?

Ehrismann's forehead is beaded with sweat.

STEWARDESS (*in English*).
Is there anything I can do for you?

Ehrismann fastens his seatbelt, pretending nothing is wrong, and tries to smile, while the stewardess, noticing the sweat on his forehead, fumbles with an air vent above his head and smiles before moving on. / The Caravelle—Swissair—from the outside. The wind sets off ripples on the wet concrete, a signalman indicates that the exit is clear, the Caravelle starts to move, slowly and laboriously, its engines, then the airport buildings, LONDON AIRPORT. Ehrismann, at his window seat. Placing the newspaper on the empty seat beside him, he unwittingly puts his pipe in his mouth.

STEWARDESS (*in English*).
No smoking, Sir.

Ehrismann immediately puts down the pipe and pretends to look out of the window—the morning sun shines on the grass, the runway signals glide by beneath the wing of the plane and we hear his voice—

5

It was too late to get off the plane and call home—

The back of his head while he looks out of the window. / A middle-aged woman, a face capable of an enigmatic beauty but now looking like it is carved in stone.

Poor Monika!

Monika is sitting, clad in a white sweater, staring, not knowing what to do. / A passenger—seatbelt fastened and waiting for take off—wants to read Ehrismann's discarded newspaper.

PASSENGER.
> May I?
> (*Ehrismann turns around.*)
> May I?

Ehrismann nods.

EHRISMANN (*in English*).
> Please.

He turns back to the window so that no one can see his face. The other passenger opens the newspaper. The picture of the burning Porsche interests him only for a moment, then he turns the page.

ANNOUNCEMENT.
> *Kapitän Hügi und seine Besatzung begrüßen Sie an Bord unsrer Caravelle. Unser Flug nach Zürich dauert eine Stunde und zehn Minuten. Danke.*
>
> (*Ehrismann looks at his watch. The announcement again, in English.*)

Captain Hügi and his crew—
(*Engine noises.*)
Thank you.
(*Crackling of the speaker.*)
We hope you'll enjoy your flight.

All the engines are on at full throttle.

Silence. A large hall—the local mortuary at the Sihlfeld cemetery. Rows of empty caskets are laid out on display.

I felt bad for Monika: the news of my death and all the trouble I couldn't help her with—

Monika in a fur coat, accompanied by her brother Willy, walking from one coffin to the next. A city official walks ahead, naming, with professional tact, a price every time Monika stops at a casket.

CITY OFFICIAL (*in Swiss dialect*).
Four hundred and ninety.

She moves on. The only sound is of her footsteps in the bleak hall.

Don't drive like a maniac. That's the last thing she said—

Monika stops.

CITY OFFICIAL (*in Swiss dialect*).
Three hundred and sixty.

Willy, the brother, does not want to get involved. He is not particular about which casket is selected but is being patient. The hall is long, the selection remarkable. Caskets with and without decoration.

CITY OFFICIAL (*in Swiss dialect*).
Two hundred and twenty.

Monika stops.

I lied. Business trip! I hadn't told anyone I was flying to London.

Monika looks at a casket, absent-mindedly. She has to pick one, after all, just not the cheapest one. She doesn't walk any further but looks across at the next one.

CITY OFFICIAL (*in Swiss dialect*).
Six hundred.

She nods, and the professionally tactful city official notes the casket number while Willy lends his arm to the widow.

Ehrismann, inside the flying Caravelle. Passengers are now allowed to unfasten their seatbelts. He does so. But what next? When the stewardess comes by with a fresh stack of newspapers, he asks for a *Neue Zürcher Zeitung*, then opens it to the obituaries as if turning to the financial or sports section, searches briefly and finds / a large obituary: 'Zurich, October 4, 1965. Theo Ehrismann, Dipl.-Ing. Our almighty God has taken . . .' / His face, while he is reading his obituary. / Then he stuffs the paper into the pocket of the seat before him.

My funeral was at eleven o'clock.

A sea of fog, sun, a cloudless sky and, across it, the gleaming wing of the plane.

I didn't know Monika was religious—she never revealed that side to me.

The ever-smiling face of the stewardess now bending towards him. She holds a tray of the usual refreshments, then folds down the table in front of him. He removes the cutlery from its plastic packaging.

I was only hoping our plane wouldn't be delayed.

Monika in front of a mirror, seen from behind. Wearing a light bathrobe, she is tentatively trying on a dark veil.

Monika in a widow's veil!

Monika takes off the veil. / Ehrismann, eating. / A black top hat being brushed by a housewife. Then the same brush, brushing a homburg. Every time, it is a different hand that brushes—a servant girl brushes black shoes, a young gentleman brushes his black pants and so on, brush on black hats, brush on black pants, brush on black shoes—the whole world is brushing. / The plane's wing above the sea of fog. / Ehrismann, in front of the small folding table now cleared. He orders a Cognac. / The mourning family in the apartment—everyone in black. Silence. The decor is conventionally modern, the furniture primarily Scandinavian, a glass coffee table, a Japanese paper lamp, a large photograph of a regatta. Everyone is drinking tea, waiting to drive to the crematorium. Willy stands and smokes a cigarette. Emmy, his wife, sits as though waiting at the dentist's. A child, apparently Emmy's, nibbles on some chocolates furtively passed to him by his mother. Gottlieb, the other brother-in-law, offers a handkerchief to his sobbing mother. Aunt Else, in horn-rimmed glasses, pours tea. A beautiful Angora cat is the only creature moving naturally, unaffectedly. Monika sits, upright and controlled. Suddenly, everyone looks to the hallway.

WILLY (*in Swiss dialect*).
Can we help you?

An old gentleman, not in mourning, stands there, slightly embarrassed. A droll figure. He realizes he is intruding but cannot remember what he came for.. He pets the cat.

GOTTLIEB (*in Swiss dialect*).
Who are you?

OLD MAN (*in Swiss dialect*).
Hofstetter.

Gottlieb has never heard of him.

OLD MAN (*in Swiss dialect*).
Hofstetter.
(*Growing increasingly uneasy.*)
I was his neighbour.

They pretend to remember and then he remembers why he has come. He approaches the widow and offers his hand.

OLD MAN (*in Swiss dialect*).
Condolences.

(Then, because he can't think of anything else to say, he shakes everyone else's hand, one after the other, even the child's.)

Condolences . . . condolences . . . condolences . . .

When there are no more hands to shake, he stands in the living room as if there is no way out. No one comes to his aid. Everyone is steeped in mournful dignity. Finally, the old man nods and simply walks away. The mourners continue to wait, motionlessly.

Airport Zurich-Kloten. The herd of passengers just arrived from London, led by a stewardess, walks across the concrete. Ehrismann in front, in a very light-coloured raincoat, no hat, holding a leather briefcase. It is raining. Ehrismann is in a hurry but the stewardess holds him back—order is of the essence. He looks around although he knows no one is expecting him. Others wave to their family or friends. / A sign: TRANSIT—ZURICH, and the stewardess, who has positioned herself beside it, asks Ehrismann.

STEWARDESS.

Transit?

(Ehrismann is perplexed—he almost turns to the wrong side just to get ahead faster.)

Zurich?

Ehrismann nods and turns to the correct side. / The face of an electrical clock—10.16. The hand twitches forward— 10.17. / Crowds milling about in the airport hall, viewed through the glass of a phone booth. Silent crowds. The reflection in the glass transforms them into shapeless masses. Ehrismann, still wearing his light raincoat, hastily dials a number. We hear the phone ring. Ehrismann waits, breathing with great effort. When someone at the other end picks up the phone, he holds his breath.

How does one say that he is alive?

He has almost lost his voice—

EHRISMANN.
    Hello—?

In the apartment, the mourning family has got to its feet, everyone in their coats and hats—a black crowd. Willy, his top hat on and the receiver at his ear, stands in the hallway and turns to one side to spare the others the interruption of the phone call.

WILLY (*in Swiss dialect*).
    Who's that? Sorry? Who's that?

He hangs up. / Ehrismann, in his light raincoat, waits a little, the receiver held to his ear, unable to believe what just happened. Then he inserts another coin, the receiver still in his hand, and re-dials. / The mourning family, on their way out. When the phone rings again, only the two brothers-in-law are left in the hallway.

My brothers-in-law never liked me, I know. I never liked them either.

They close the apartment door behind them and let the phone ring. / Ehrismann, as before, the receiver against his ear. Finally, he hangs up, thinks for a moment, glances at his watch, picks up his briefcase and leaves the phone booth. / The three cars of the mourning family moving through the traffic. / Ehrismann, in a taxi. He sits upright, he cannot relax. The briefcase is on his knees. Folk music plays on the radio.

EHRISMANN.
 Crematorium.
 (*The driver turns off the radio.*)
 Crematorium.

The driver, after he has heard Ehrismann, turns the radio on again, this time at full volume. Ehrismann in his light raincoat, the briefcase on his knee, starts stuffing his pipe, to do something about the red traffic lights.

The silence of a graveyard. A rake on a gravel path covered with fallen leaves. It is still raining. An Art Nouveau gate. At the end of an alley we see the dome of the crematorium. A grey day with no horizon in sight. There is no one around, except for the gardener raking leaves. / Then, Ehrismann in his light raincoat. He comes through the Art Nouveau gate and walks along the middle of the main road, leather briefcase in hand, as if on his way to a professional meeting. / A look back down the alley—it is empty.

I was the first one there. Or the ceremony had already started—

His face, the pipe in his mouth. / He walks through the alley, faster now. A parking sign: 'P for Mourning Families Only'. Although the parking lot is empty, Ehrismann steps to one side and continues walking behind a high hedge.

Now he is almost running until he sees a woman at a grave bunching flowers into a can. He immediately slows down in order to suit the solemnity of the location. / View into a courtyard—rain in the water-lily pond, cypresses behind bleak arcades. Nobody here either. / Ehrismann, in his light raincoat, walks up the front steps. Without hesitation—not solemn but straightforward. At the open door he at least takes the pipe out of his mouth. Then walks along the empty pews, his steps echoing in the room. Then silence. Ehrismann stands—leather briefcase under his left arm and pipe in his right hand—in front of a casket covered by ribboned wreaths.

> *Theo Ehrismann. Remembered. Family Korrodi-Weber. Rest in Peace. / In Memory of Our Theo Ehrismann. Studer Electronics. / Good-Bye. Willy and Else Escher-Tobler and their Children. / To Its Founder and Patron Theo Ehrismann: Yacht Club Turicum. / . . .*

His face—neither moved nor amused. His mind—a blank. He turns to leave—there is nothing left to do here. On the stairs he puts the pipe back in his mouth. It has gone out and he has to light it again. / View down the alley—the first guests are arriving in the distance, with umbrellas, in groups and singly, all of them walking unnaturally slowly.

> *I was the only one in a light-coloured raincoat.*

It is a few moments before they come closer.

> *Of course I wanted to make myself seen—that was my duty—I wanted to make myself seen and tell them that I was alive—*

It is a while before the mourners approach. / Ehrismann, hiding behind the high hedge, smokes his pipe quickly and furtively. He can only see a small part of the alley and the first mourner to come into view is an elderly gentleman, walking with a cane. He has no umbrella.

My former mathematics teacher, whom we used to call Copernicus, I didn't know he was still around.

Three women pass by.

Neighbours. They've always been keen on hearing my curriculum vitae.

A gentleman with an umbrella.

My tax accountant.

A woman with two children.

Frau Hubalek, our cleaning lady.

No one else comes along for a while.

My parents are dead, my sister's in Chile—I hope she didn't make an unnecessary trip halfway around the world.

A young woman comes by.

Fräulein Steiner, my secretary.

A young man.

He came because of Monika.

The young man is clad in impeccable mourning attire. / A rear view of Ehrismann—stretching behind the hedge, trying to get a better view of the young man. Suddenly, he is gripped by curiousity. / A view of the young man. A slender—much more than Ehrismann—playboy with an intellectual touch, now wearing an expression of grave seriousness.

So that's what he looks like, the young man who under-stands my Monika so well and who has been doing so for the past year and a half.

The rear view continues. The young man walks even more slowly than two other mourning guests who pass him by without a greeting.

Must have been a hard day for him too. I can relate to him. Now Monika will be free.

Again, the view of the alley as before. Suddenly, there are many people, a whole flock, in black.

I didn't expect that, I have to admit. So many—

Ehrismann places his briefcase on the wet earth near the trunk of a cypress, the pipe still in his mouth.

I was touched.

Two men wearing homburgs.

Studer Electronics. Well—

Here and there, the mourning guests greet each other with a silent nod of their heads. Nobody speaks. All we hear is the crunch of their shoes on the gravel path. Once in a while we see the smoke from Ehrismann's pipe wafting up from behind the hedge. For a while nobody else comes by.

Barbara didn't come.

A group of younger men.

Yacht Club Turicum.

Then, quite a few people pass by about whom Ehrismann is silent. / His face—wet from the rain since he is hatless. Smoking his pipe, he is detached yet curious. / Three Swiss officers in uniform pass by—Commanding Officer, Major, Colonel. The first among the mourners who don't look at the ground but straight ahead.

I'd been an officer too.

Now, finally, the three cars of the mourning family, shiny and black, moving as slowly as the pedestrians. They stop without a sound at the sign: 'P for Mourning Families Only'. The pedestrians, who want to stand and stare, keep walking—it would be indecent to peer at the family as if they were stars.

I was determined to reveal myself. I was only waiting for Monika. I was determined.

It is a while before the car doors open. Everything happens slowly. Men emerge, top hats, umbrellas are opened, then the ladies follow. Everyone stands around.

The members of the Escher family by themselves again.

More standing around.

Why don't they come?

A single person walks by.

Viktor!

Obviously an outsider, Viktor wears a Basque hat and a dark—not black—coat. No tie, no gloves. Viktor does not look to the ground either. He is solemn but detached.

Why haven't we seen each other for years? I don't know. A man doesn't have many friends—

Nobody comes along for a while.

So Barbara really didn't come.

Then—footsteps on the gravel.

Monika!

Monika, as a widow, supported by her two brothers, slowly walks by.

Why I didn't step out of my hiding place then I don't know—

Monika as widow. Upright and calm, her face Madonna-like under the veil, dignified. / Ehrismann, behind the hedge. He now takes the pipe out of his mouth and puts it away in his pocket, as though it is something indecent.

That was a mistake: I put away my pipe as if I believed in my own funeral. That was the first mistake.

The sound of an organ, and the open portal of the crematorium. Team Monika walks up the steps and disappears into the building / while Ehrismann steps out of his hiding place, without his briefcase, and enters the alley, following the congregation. / Two funeral officials shut the heavy door so that the organ music is suddenly muted. They leave it closed when they see Ehrismann—no one attends a crematorium in a light raincoat. / Rain splashes in the water-lily pond. The organ plays on. / Two latecomers, having to walk around the pond, are in a hurry and don't take notice of the deceased sitting by the edge of the water. They run up the steps, top hats in hand. Only when the doors open do they adopt the more dignified walk appropriate to the occasion. A flood of droning organ sounds until the doors close again.

Go on, go ahead without me!

Ehrismann stands up and leaves. / Hands holding black gloves, black shoes under the pews. The organ is silent. The voice of a Protestant minister.

MINISTER.
Let us pray!

The sound of creaking pews. / Ehrismann knocks on the wet window of a black limousine. Seen through the glass, his face no longer looks like it belongs to a gentleman.

I was wondering where the congregation would gather after the funeral.

The driver rolls down his window.

DRIVER.
Restaurant 'Eintracht'.

The driver rolls his window back up / and Ehrismann leaves, hands in his raincoat pockets, along the empty alley, when he hears someone addressing him.

VOICE.

Are you from Zurich?

Ehrismann turns around.

EHRISMANN.

Why?

The gentleman is a mourner wearing a black homburg. He is anxious since he is running late. When he speaks, it is in the fast, harsh and clear German of Hamburg.

STRANGER.

You wouldn't know where the Zurich crematorium is? There are no signs anywhere.

(*Ehrismann turns up the collar of his coat.*)

Is the funeral over?

EHRISMANN.

Whose funeral?

STRANGER.

Engineer Ehrismann's.

EHRISMANN.

Straight ahead.

STRANGER.

Thank you.

EHRISMANN.

You're welcome.

STRANGER.

You're not going?

EHRISMANN.

I'd rather not.

The minister on the pulpit.

MINISTER.

Amen.—

(*A good-natured face, Protestant, middle-class, devoid of anything mystical. Very correct. He picks up a Bible, a small one, and waits until the pews have stopped creaking. He reads with a dialect-inflected intonation and without any pathos, almost as if he is reading out a bulletin.*)

'Whether then it was I or they, so we preach, and so you believed. Corinthians 15:11.'

(*He puts the Bible aside.*)

Dear congregation—

The sound of boys yelling—we don't see them right away. A field somewhere on the outskirts of the city. Three scattered apartment buildings tower over a desert of allotment gardens. A construction site. A crane. A rattling concrete mixer. Ehrismann, in his light raincoat, has stopped to watch, a leisurely spectator. Boys play soccer between the barracks. In the background, we can hear—

VOICE OF THE MINISTER.

Almighty God has called from this life to the eternal life—Theo Ehrismann, born in Zurich on April the 11th, 1924, only son of Ignaz Ehrismann, innkeeper, and of Luise Ehrismann Nägeli, certified engineer, married to Dorothea Monika Ehrismann, née Escher—

The ball lands beyond the wire fence and rolls onto the street. Ehrismann runs after it but one of the boys is quicker. Ehrismann strolls on, hands in his pockets, relaxed, while work continues on the construction site. In the background, we can hear—

VOICE OF THE MINISTER.
> Almighty God—certified engineer in eternity—married in eternity—Theo Ehrismann in eternity—

The rattling of the concrete mixer.

> *I was happy I didn't have to listen to this. I felt bad for the minister. He was describing a man he'd never met.*

A truck pours out gravel. / Monika as widow in the first row, tears in her eyes.

VOICE OF THE MINISTER.
> So let us in this dark hour look once again upon a life that has passed on to eternity, dear congregation, just as we will pass on to eternity.

Pause, then the organ starts to play, / while Ehrismann, in his light raincoat, strolls further. / On the choir balcony a large lady begins to sing, music sheet in hand. A performance fit for a concert, and she is completely focused on the music. / While we hear the Bach cantata, we see the street with puddles, a rusty can. Ehrismann kicks it, soccer-style, but it rolls only a little distance away and then stops. Ehrismann tries to dribble with it, as if he is circling a defender, but the can rolls away and he misses his kick. Only now taking his hands out of his pockets, he starts to run for a penalty kick. He was once able to do this but he is no longer a boy—his breathing grows hard and heavy but he won't give up. Ambition has grabbed him, and, finally, he manages a full kick—the can whirls in a high arc sideways across the field and we hear a shrill clattering on top of the Bach cantata. / Silence. The dirty window of an allotment garden cabin. The glass is shattered. Rain, spiderwebs, broken glass. / The widow, now in front of the crematorium entrance, receiving condolences from: the three neighbours, the accountant, the cleaning lady and her children, the secretary, the gentlemen from the Yacht Club Turicum. They offer their hands in silence. Her veiled face is dignified-beautiful as she is confronted with so much sympathy.

The hissing sound of an espresso machine. We are on the first floor of the restaurant 'Eintracht', a bar with a suburban flair. Voices, the rattling of dishes. The guests are workers and minor white-collar employees. An Italian waitress by the espresso machine, Ehrismann sits at the bar, still in his light raincoat.

> *I didn't know what they were doing for so long. I was determined—*
> (*He downs a Grappa.*)
> *I was still determined.*
> (*The hissing of the espresso machine.*)
> *They won't believe their eyes!*
> (*He orders a second Grappa.*)

WAITER (*in Italian*).
Where are the buns?

WAITRESS (*in Italian*).
Buns!

The hissing of the espresso machine.

WAITER (*in Italian*).
Buns!

The waiter, who nervously squeezes in behind the bar, looks like he is dressed up in a costume, *comme il faut*. He doesn't belong to the bar but with the guests on the second floor. He takes the basket of fresh buns arrived from the kitchen and disappears. / The dining hall on the second floor—a horseshoe-shaped table. *Comme il faut.* The waiter places a bun at each place setting. Plates full of cold meats, a whole battery of wine bottles. The waiter looks across the table to see if everything is ready for the mourning guests. / Ehrismann downs his second Grappa, staring straight ahead. He doesn't take notice of the Italian guest-worker gesturing theatrically and trying to get money out of someone.

GUEST WORKER (*in Italian*).
Dead! Dead! My wife. You understand? Dead. And I— no money. You understand? No francs—
(*He has tears in his eyes. No one wants to hear him out or heed his plight, not even when he pulls out a yellowish photograph from his pocket*—)
That's her. Look! My fiancé. Dead. Her. Dead. Tomorrow is the funeral. Look! She—
(*Nobody wants to look at the photograph.*)
The Swiss never understand anything!

24

(He wears his striped Sunday suit, a white shirt with a high collar, a tie. He seems to be well known here. Finally, he turns to Ehrismann.)

Signore—

The waiter pushes him away.

WAITER *(in Italian).*

That's enough! Enough now!

Ehrismann hasn't noticed a thing. He holds his empty Grappa glass, sweat beading on his forehead. He stares, the Grappa glass drops from his hand, with a crash / but it is the crash of the window from earlier. The old mathematics teacher known as Copernicus looks out from inside the cabin with the broken window and crooks his finger, the way a friendly teacher beckons an unruly student. / The hissing of the espresso machine. Suddenly it is no longer the Italian waitress serving at the bar but Monika. She points her finger at Ehrismann. / The organ plays. A big metal gate opens—the premises of Studer Electronics. The two gentlemen Studer carry a tiny coffin, smaller than a child's, across the courtyard. In front of the gate is a company standing to attention, led by the three helmeted officers also standing to attention. They all wear helmets and martial attitudes. As the tiny casket is carried across the courtyard, the whole company bursts out laughing. / And while we hear the laughter, we see a sailboat capsizing in Lake Zurich. / The two brothers-in-law, top-hatted and wearing black, stand on the quay, grinning, throwing wreaths instead of life vests. / The smile of the stewardess. / Another woman, Barbara, sitting in a bathtub, holding a whisky glass and laughing.

25

I felt dizzy.

Ehrismann, his eyes closed. When he opens them again, / we see the espresso machine hissing, the Italian waitress, the guests drinking beer or eating soup. Everything is back to normal. No one takes note of Ehrismann at all—nothing seems out of the ordinary. / The coat racks on the second floor. We can't see the people, only hands reaching out to hang up a top hat or a homburg—

VOICES (*in Swiss dialect*).

How time passes . . . That's what I'd say . . . She's got a grown-up daughter now as well . . . May I introduce myself . . . Who would have thought . . . Do you also have such bad weather? . . . Sad, such a young wife . . . How long will you be in Zurich for? . . .

—until the rack is full. / Ehrismann slowly walks between the tables towards a jukebox.

Suddenly I felt like listening to music.

He stands in front of the jukebox, still in his light raincoat, his hand searching in his pocket for a coin while he studies the list of available Schlager songs. / The dining hall on the second floor. The mourners are seated, embarrassed, quiet, stiff, a black crowd in the white room, taxidermized. Only the two waiters move—one pours wine; the other arrives with a plate full of cold cuts. The mourners begin to serve themselves after the first few moments of appropriate hesitation. Silence. / The jukebox. Ehrismann inserts a coin, presses a button, then another, then a third. / The minister picks up his wine glass but not before glancing at the widow seated beside him.

MINISTER (*in Swiss dialect*).
Frau Ehrisma—

The widow, too, picks up her glass. She only sips from it, while the minister, in order to defuse the generally awkward mood, takes a full sip, then, tasting the liquor, another.

MINISTER (*in Swiss dialect*).
Is this a Hallauer?

WILLY (*whispers, in Swiss dialect*).
His favourite.

Everyone else is as stiff as a mummy. Now the jukebox from downstairs can be heard, not very loud but clear—Edith Piaf is singing.

JUKEBOX.
'*No, rien de rien,*
non, je ne regrette rien,
ni le bien qu'on m'a fait,
ni le mal,
tout ça m'est bien egal', etc.

The minister pretends he cannot hear and begins to eat. The widow has apparently not heard anything. The others have but don't pay any attention and begin to break their bread. / Ehrismann, by the illuminated jukebox which we can now hear at full volume.

JUKEBOX.
'*Avec mes souvenirs*
j'ai allume le feu,
mes chargrins, mes plaisirs
je n'ai plus besoin d'eux', etc.

Ehrismann, in his light raincoat, leaning against the juke-box, now enjoying himself—it couldn't be loud enough for him. / The waiter, hand on the bannister, races down the stairs to reprimand the drunk.

JUKEBOX.
   '*Non, rien de rien,*
   non, je ne regrette rien', etc.

We can't hear what the waiter says—a pantomime plays out as he points to the upstairs and protests on behalf of the mourners. Ehrismann is unimpressed and unmoved. The song ends.

WAITER (*in French*).
   Enough now!

The waiter pushes Ehrismann away from the jukebox. Ehrismann doesn't resist and sits down at the next table where some people are eating their soup and who remain oblivious of him. / Close-up of the inexorable mechanics of the record changer after the waiter has left. Then, again at full volume.

JUKEBOX.
   'Oh, when the saints go marchin' in.'

Close-up of the minister's face. He listens, ostentatiously outraged. / Close-up of the widow's face—her dignity is holding up. / Close-up of Viktor's face—he is secretly amused. / Close-up of the mother-in-law's face—she looks accusingly at her sons, who chose this restaurant. / The waiter can only shrug. / One of the gentlemen Studer, intending to start a little speech on behalf of the company, is standing, notes in hand, waiting for Louis Armstrong to finish.

STUDER.
   Dear bereaved—

The hissing of the espresso machine. Ehrismann, at the table of soup-eaters, loosens his tie and collar. He is miserable, breathing with his mouth open. / The inexorable mechanism of the record changer, then Piaf again.

JUKEBOX.
   '*Allez, venez, Milord!*'

Ehrismann is no longer listening, and has broken into a sweat. One of the soup-eaters notices and tries giving some helpful advice. Ehrismann is now as white as a sheet.

JUKEBOX.
   '*Allez, venez, Milord!*'

Ehrismann gets to his feet. People make way for him as though he is someone in sudden need of throwing up. Outside in the stairway, where the music is especially loud, he has to hold on to the bannister for support. For a while it seems he wants to sit down on the stairs.

JUKEBOX.
   '*Allez, venez, Milord!*'

Ehrismann, in his light raincoat, staggers up the stairs. / The coat racks on the second floor. The black hats, the black coats, the black umbrellas. Beside it, the door to the dining hall. A sign—'Reserved'. Ehrismann carefully opens the door a crack but doesn't enter.

JUKEBOX.
   'Mais vous pleurez, Milord? ça je l'aurais jamais cru.'

Rear view of Ehrismann, spying through the gap in the door. But the table is not visible. / Inside, Studer is standing, silent, notes in hand. Everyone turns towards the door through which the music can be heard, now louder.

JUKEBOX.
   'Mais oui, dansez, Milord!'

Now that's enough—the minister gets up, strides around the horseshoe table, while the *chanson* grows more and more bombastic, and approaches the door. / Ehrismann, outside. The face of the minister appears at the door. He never knew the deceased and thus regards this man as a drunk, a mischief-maker. The wordless singing of Piaf, her invitation to dance, then the slamming of the door, then silence. The sign on the door: 'Reserved'. One of the two waiters arrives with coffee.

WAITER 2 (*in Swiss dialect*).
   Where to?

EHRISMANN.
   Toilette.

The waiter indicates where to go with a jerk of his head.

WAITER 2 (*in Swiss dialect*).
   But you still need to pay!

The waiter with the coffee goes into the dining hall. / Another door with a sign: 'Gentlemen'. Ehrismann enters, after ensuring it is unoccupied. / Inside the hall, things are now proceeding smoothly. The waiter pours coffee. The guests are less stiff.

VIKTOR (*in Swiss dialect*).
Sugar?

Studer takes some, then Viktor passes the sugar bowl to his other side.

VIKTOR (*in Swiss dialect*).
Sugar?

A lady takes some, then passes the bowl.

LADY (*in Swiss dialect*).
Do you take sugar?

Ehrismann in the toilet. Kneeling beside the toilet bowl after vomiting, he wipes his mouth with toilet paper. Someone rattles the locked door to the stall. Ehrismann holds his breath—he doesn't dare throw up again. / Outside, the suffering man rattles the door once more, then gives up and goes across to the mirror, combs his hair, looks at his watch. / Close-up of Ehrismann's face—he is terrified.

My briefcase! Suddenly I noticed I'd left my briefcase somewhere—

His leather briefcase at the cemetery. Autumn leaves. The leaves of the cypress dripping rain. / Ehrismann, still kneeling in the toilet, fixes his tie. Voices in the hallway. He listens. / Through the keyhole, a cropped view of two black-clad gentlemen standing next to each other at the urinals. We hear them without seeing their heads.

FIRST MAN (*in Swiss dialect*).
This evening.

SECOND MAN (*in Swiss dialect*).
Who's playing?

FIRST MAN (*in Swiss dialect*).
Switzerland–Czechoslovakia.

They piss.

SECOND MAN (*in Swiss dialect*).
Oh, our Teddy!

They wash their hands.

FIRST MAN (*in Swiss dialect*).
Oh, our Teddy!

SECOND MAN (*in Swiss dialect*).
The Porsche is a dangerous car. That's what I've always said. A racy car but dangerous.

FIRST MAN (*in Swiss dialect*).
What do you drive now?

SECOND MAN (*in Swiss dialect*).
My Citroen still.

They dry their hands, then move outside the keyhole view. One of them unwittingly whistles a few bars of 'Milord'. / Close-up of Ehrismann's face while the whistling grows distorted—the echo of an unreal space— / the site of the accident, how it was shown in the newspapers, with the burning Porsche but in bright daylight. No police, no ambulance, no onlookers. Instead the black figures of the mourning congregation watching the car burn. Everybody seen from behind, everybody standing in quiet devotion to the black smoke rising from the burning Porsche.

EHRISMANN.

Gottlieb—!

(*We hear the crackling of the fire.*)

Willy—!

(*They can't hear him.*)

Hello—!

(*He kneels on the bright street, in his light raincoat, twenty metres behind the mourners.*)

Monika?

(*She is standing, propped between her two brothers, her black veil blowing in the wind.*)

Hello.

Finally, Willy turns around, annoyed by the interruption. He speaks quietly, as if Ehrismann is standing very close to him.

WILLY.

What is it?

Willy shakes his head, disapproving of such impossible behaviour—he can't deal with it right now—and turns back to the burning Porsche.

EHRISMANN.

Monika!

(*Now Gottlieb turns around.*)

Gottlieb—

33

Gottlieb expresses sympathy in the manner of comforting someone who turned out to be his own worst enemy. He whispers, trying not to cause a commotion.

GOTTLIEB (*in Swiss dialect*).
You can't do that. What are you thinking? You can't do that.

Both of them turn back to the burning car. / Close-up of Ehrismann's face—kneeling on the street, he is hit by the full force of his powerlessness. He gets up to leave. / Ehrismann steps out of the toilet, listens. We can hear muffled laughter from inside the hall. Ehrismann walks downstairs. / Inside the hall, the guests have loosened up. Some have left, others have gathered in groups. In the foreground, three men with cigars.

ONE OF THEM (*in Swiss dialect*).
Know the joke about the Jew who got into Heaven?

They smoke for a bit for camouflage.

ONE OF THEM (*in Swiss dialect*).
A Jew got into Heaven—

He whispers so that the widow can't hear him. She now sits beside Viktor. Since she is silent, Viktor feels the need to say something. He fiddles with the glass in front of him.

VIKTOR (*in Swiss dialect*).
I liked him well. Yes, I liked him well—

Now the laughter of the men, short and loud and then abruptly cut off. Cigar smoke. / Silence. The rake on the cemetery gravel strewn with autumn leaves. The rain has stopped. Ehrismann, in his light raincoat, is looking for his briefcase.

Hopefully nobody'd found my briefcase. That's all I needed, to have the police be looking for me now—

He finds it leaning against the cypress, picks it up, then looks back again down the alley at the dome of the crematorium. / An employee inside—working with an expert and sober professionalism—engraving a small sign to be attached to the urn: 'Theo Ehrismann, October 7, 1965'.

The employee is wearing a grey jumpsuit. / Ehrismann looks around, checks if any one can see him. He needs to wait. / View into a pit that could be a grave—planks, a shovel, a dull pool of water at the bottom of the pit into which the briefcase is dropped with a splash. / Ehrismann's shoes as he kicks dirt over the briefcase. / His face, as if nothing has happened. While he walks away / we see that it is no grave but a pit at a construction site. The workers pay no attention to the leisurely passer-by. / Traffic on the Badenerstrasse (a main street leading through a working-class neighbourhood into the city). Ehrismann sees the man with the black homburg waving at a taxi—

STRANGER.
     Taxi!

The man, who came from abroad for my sake—

STRANGER.
     Taxi!

EHRISMANN.

Can I help you?

STRANGER.

Aren't there any taxis around here?

Ehrismann, smoking his pipe, stands beside the unknown mourner who is apparently in a hurry, and helps him look for a taxi.

EHRISMANN.

How was the funeral?

(*The stranger appears preoccupied.*)

Got there on time?

STRANGER.

Thank you, yes, thank you.

EHRISMANN.

How was it, anyway?

(*Still no taxis in sight.*)

Where do you need to go?

STRANGER.

Studer Electronics.

They continue to wait.

A modern office. Employees sit at their computers under a neon-light brightness. The secretary has taken her boss' black coat. Studer washes his hands.

SECRETARY (*in Swiss dialect*).

The gentlemen are waiting.

Studer dries his hands. / A conference room. Five men are waiting, one of whom is reading the *New York Times*. When Studer enters, they stand up with the evident nonchalance of those who have arrived on time.

STUDER (*in English*).
    I beg your pardon. I'm very sorry, gentlemen, for being so late.
    (*Everyone sits down. Dossiers are opened. The meeting is about to begin.*)
    (*In English—*)
    Mister Ehrismann, supposed to do this business, is no longer with us. You know he died the other day.
    (*Pause. Then, in English—*)
    Well.—

Ehrismann, in his light raincoat, and the stranger with the black homburg, walk down Badenerstrasse. Their faces, side by side. Ehrismann is now wearing his sunglasses.

STRANGER.
    Didn't know he was an excellent sailor—

EHRISMANN.
    Oh.

STRANGER.
    An Olympic sailor.

EHRISMANN.
    That was a long time ago.

They walk.

STRANGER.

I appreciated him as a specialist.

EHRISMANN.

I see.

STRANGER.

Very much.

EHRISMANN.

Did you actually know him?

STRANGER.

Only through correspondence.

(*Ehrismann turns to look at the stranger.*)

And such a young wife.

EHRISMANN.

You think so?

STRANGER.

Tragic.

EHRISMANN.

She seemed very composed to me.

STRANGER.

Very.

EHRISMANN.

Wasn't she?

STRANGER.

Wonderful.

(*Pause.*)

Fortunately, they have no kids—

EHRISMANN.

Only a cat.

STRANGER.

—They say it was a happy marriage, though.

EHRISMANN.

I didn't know that.

STRANGER.

So they say.

They cross a side street. We see them from behind and cannot hear what they are saying. Then, the two faces, side by side, seen from the front—

EHRISMANN.

It's possible he told me about you, perhaps I'll remember if you tell me your name—

STRANGER.

Maschke.

EHRISMANN.

That's you?!

MASCHKE.

Hamburg. General dealership representation for Germany.

EHRISMANN.

I know, Herr Maschke.

MASCHKE.

We used to correspond a lot.

(For a moment Ehrismann thinks he's been recognized but then realizes that Maschke is talking about the dead.)
You were a friend?

EHRISMANN.
—Kind of . . . not always . . . how should I put it?—I went to school with him . . .

MASCHKE.
Oh yes?

EHRISMANN.
Yes.

Pause.

MASCHKE.
I wonder who his successor will be.

EHRISMANN.
I don't.

Maschke stops to light a cigarette but his lighter doesn't work. Ehrismann helps out with a matchbox.

MASCHKE.
Director Studer spoke beautifully—

EHRISMANN.
He did.

MASCHKE.
Short but heartfelt.
(The cigarette is alight.)
Thank you.

EHRISMANN.

I can't handle funeral speeches.

MASCHKE.

I understand. They always make us think of ourselves.
I'm the same. I listen and can't help thinking— suddenly it all goes on without you . . .
(*Ehrismann nods politely.*)
You live in Zurich?

EHRISMANN.

I live in Zurich.

MASCHKE.

Too bad.

EHRISMANN.

Why?

MASCHKE.

That I never met this man. You understand, personally.

EHRISMANN.

I understand.

MASCHKE.

A shame.

Pause. They walk, and the pause grows longer and longer.
Again and again Maschke looks for a taxi. In vain. As Ehrismann takes off his dark sunglasses, the words are out before
he can stop himself—

EHRISMANN.

Herr Maschke—

(*He stops.*)

Herr Maschke, may I invite you to a glass of Fendant?

MASCHKE.

What's that?

EHRISMANN.

A Swiss wine.

MASCHKE.

That's very kind—

EHRISMANN.

A light one, but pretty good.

(*Maschke wants to keep walking.*)

Come on! That's the best we can do. Let's drink to the engineer!

- (*He laughs.*)

May his ashes rest in peace!

MASCHKE.

That's very kind—

Ehrismann takes his arm.

EHRISMANN.

Come on, Herr Maschke, let's go!

It's an embarrassing situation and Ehrismann can sense it—he is becoming too jovial, Maschke is a gentleman who doesn't like to be taken by the arm. He is uncomfortable, until Ehrismann takes his hand away.

MASCHKE.

Unfortunately, I still have to go by Studer Electronics, you understand—

EHRISMANN.

Why 'have to'?

MASCHKE.

Business trip.

(*He waves in the direction of the street.*)

Taxi!

EHRISMANN.

I see. You didn't come to Zurich just to attend a funeral—

MASCHKE.

Taxi!

A taxi stops.

EHRISMANN.

Herr Maschke—

MASCHKE.

Herr—?

EHRISMANN.

Don't mention it, Herr Maschke, don't mention it, it was my pleasure.

Ehrismann in the street, in his light raincoat, as before. Aimless, after Maschke's refusal.

I had more time than ever before.

Ehrismann in front of a wall with posters.

As if I was in a foreign city.

Ehrismann at a roasted-chestnut vendor.

I started to get hungry.

Ehrismann in front of a movie theatre, eating chestnuts.

I didn't feel like it.

Ehrismann in front of a shop window, eating chestnuts.

When I saw the bookstore where Barbara worked I didn't feel like that either. What for? I didn't want to be seen—

He walks on. / Barbara, inside the bookstore, with a customer who cannot make up his mind. The man puts down the book he is holding. Barbara is very friendly. The customer nods, so does she. As the man leaves, we see Ehrismann through the open door. He crosses the street, convinced he has not been seen. It takes Barbara three seconds before she can believe her eyes, then she rushes out onto the street and almost into a car that stops in the nick of time. Nothing happens, but she freezes in her tracks, stunned, letting the angry driver yell at her.

DRIVER (*in Swiss dialect*).
    Are you crazy?

She has to think this through. Because Ehrismann is no longer visible, she runs back into the store and grabs her coat and umbrella.

BARBARA (*in Swiss dialect*).

He's alive—alive—

Fighting the urge to rush out the door, she runs to the phone, almost begins to dial a number but doesn't have the patience, drops the receiver on the table and runs out the door without bothering to shut it behind her. Barbara on the street. Running, walking quickly, running again. Her face. Doubtful one moment, then not the next. He has long disappeared—which way should she go? She runs in one direction, then in another. It is pointless, she realizes, and gets onto a streetcar.

A skeleton in a Celtic grave. The skull is not quite intact, the vertebrae and the ribs are sunk into the clay, bones from the feet lie scattered, the pelvic bone is awry and so on. The grave suddenly seen inside a display case, its glass reflecting the spectator—Ehrismann, in his light raincoat. / He is disparaging, amused. As if Chance had come up with a cliché for a punchline. / Then he wanders further through the hall—full of glass cases—without looking at anything too closely, into the next.

> *Here I was sure I wouldn't meet anyone I knew. Who would ever go to the National Museum! I hadn't been there for at least twenty years.*

The silence of a museum. The objects that must not be touched. The brightness of a hospital. The visitors turn silent too. Timelessness. / Ehrismann, standing before a barge from the logger era. He is not really looking at any of the exhibits—merely pretending.

45

Hopefully Barbara didn't see me.

He wanders further. / Traffic. Barbara, not giving up, searching in the crowds, / while Ehrismann sits down in yet another hall, his hands thrust into his coat pockets. Since there is nothing else to do, he finds himself slowly focusing on the objects that surround him, although not yet moving from his position on the bench. A wall with Roman fragments from the forum of Martigny, a bull's head made of bronze, the leg of the same bull, a man's arm in bronze, a man's thigh in bronze, everything quite beautiful. Silence. At one point, voices from a group of schoolchildren who pass through the hall. Silence. Ehrismann gets up in order to read the labels. / Traffic. Barbara at a traffic light, forced to wait. The three black cars of the mourning family on their way home. When the light changes, Barbara doesn't move, / while Ehrismann wanders through hall after hall. Weapons and flags of the Swiss. He stops—the helmet and the sword of Ulrich Zwingli. He reads the label, then his gaze wanders again, here and there. He stands by a window.

The Museum will close at four. Then what? The rain's stopped.

He stops. / One of the black cars stops in front of the house. The driver gets out to open the door. A few seconds later the two brothers-in-law step out, followed by the widow.

It's my duty to go home—

The brothers-in-law accompany the widow into the house. / Ehrismann, in his light raincoat, still stands by the window of the Museum—

Perhaps it'll be a celebration.

A guard walks by. / Close-up of Ehrismann, slowly beginning to enjoy the idea: / Monika in a white evening gown, *décolleté,* and wearing jewellery, placing two Burgundy glasses on a table. Ehrismann in a suit, an Italian maid handing him a bottle-opener.

EHRISMANN (*in Italian*).
How are you?

MAID (*in Italian*).
Signore—

EHRISMANN (*in Italian*).
Everything all right?

MAID (*in Italian*).
Oh my god—

EHRISMANN.
(*Beginning in Italian*) A miracle, isn't it?
(*He carefully opens a Burgundy.*)
You're right, Monika—no more sports cars. I swear! And never again a business trip that my Monika doesn't know of!
(*He smells the cork.*)
You have my word!
(*They look at each other.*)
And not another question about Barbara. Promise? No more questions from me either.
(*He fills the two glasses.*)

Honour the secret of your neighbour that you may live long with him!

(*They raise a toast.*)

It's good that we've finally talked. Finally. How can a couple be so childish for eleven years—

(*The doorbell rings.*)

Prosit!

(*The bell rings again. They look to the door but don't move to open it. Clearly, they want to be alone.*)

Monika, I'd like to apologize.

(*The bell rings again. Ehrismann goes to the door: it's Viktor, a bottle of Chianti in his hands.*)

Viktor!

VIKTOR.

Some joke!

They embrace.

EHRISMANN.

You know my wife?

(*Viktor nods and offers his hand.*)

You don't know her!

The bell rings again and this time Monika goes to open the door.

EHRISMANN.

I told her everything.

VIKTOR.

What?

EHRISMANN.

Everything. That you think she's a prima donna, a diva who's in love with herself, that I'm an asshole. Take off your coat!

(*The voices of many people.*)

Don't you remember? When I married her? 'Asshole!' you said. Literally. That's why we haven't seen each other for eleven years, my friend—

VIKTOR.

You told her that?

Monika joins them.

EHRISMANN.

Look at her!

(*The gentlemen from the Yacht Club are here to celebrate his resurrection, each holding a whisky bottle and accompanied by an evening gown-clad young lady.*)

Ahoy!

(*He lifts his glass.*)

Welcome mateys! I've seen your grief. I thank you. We will sail on.

(*The bell rings again.*)

Let's just leave the door open!

In the hallway is the bewidlered old man, as awkward and embarrassed as before. He offers his hand to the widow—

OLD MAN.

Congratulations—

(*Then he shakes everybody's hand, except Ehrismann's.
Also of each of the girls' accompanying the Yacht Club
men.*)

Congratulations—congratulations—

More and more people turn up. Then the crowd begins to
dance. The two Studers arrive as does Herr Maschke—all
three still in their black mourning attire and the only ones,
by the way, without gifts. Ehrismann greets them as he
dances and without letting go of Monika.

EHRISMANN.

I can see, gentlemen, that you've already found my successor.

(*Embarrassment.*)

Herr Maschke, I congratulate you.

(*They stand there while he dances on.*)

It was time for me to change, it was time . . .

(*Everyone mills about. / Silence in the National Museum.
Ehrismann, in his light raincoat, standing by the window
and being watched by the guard. Ehrismann can sense it—
he needs to move on and not become conspicuous. / Ehrismann in front of an early mediaeval wooden Madonna in
which he isn't the slightest bit interested. He is only pretending, earning himself some time—*)

It could also be very different.

(*He stops / when he sees the widow at home. Monika, the
suspicious wife, sitting in silence.*)

I was in London. That's all. And now I'm here—

(*Ehrismann takes off his light raincoat, upset and grim, while she pours some of the tea left over from the funeral guests—which is presumably not only cold but also bitter. He sits down.*)

I know, Monika, what you went through. I'm sorry.

(*He tries to joke.*)

Almighty God has taken—Amen—just as we will enter eternity—

(*But the joke fails, and the tea is undrinkable. Ehrismann looks around—an apartment full of flowers and a bitter wife.*)

So this is what it's like when one comes back to life—

(*He gets up, walks over to the bar in need of a drink, says nothing in order not to say anything inappropriate, takes the bottle and fills a small glass and discreetly checks if Monika is crying.*)

I thought you'd be happy that I'm not dead. But the moment I'm back it's the same old song.

(*He downs the schnapps.*)

Why London? You don't believe me. Well, don't. I've said it before—it wasn't a business trip—

(*Monika starts to cry.*)

Can't you understand that?

(*He waits until she controls her tears.*)

All of a sudden I found myself thinking—why a business trip? Ridiculous. I felt like going to London. Why don't we just live? That's all—I felt like going to London—

(*Monika starts crying again.*)

For god's sake!

(*His self-control is all used up. He hurls the small glass to the floor, is immediately ashamed and wants to apologize but can't. He tries hard to speak calmly and patiently.*)

It isn't my fault that someone took my car and drove himself to death—the poor bugger . . .

(*He puts the pipe in his mouth.*)

What's that got to do with Barbara?

(*Then, suddenly, he bursts out—*)

I was not with Barbara!

(*Silence in the room. / Silence in the National Museum. Ehrismann in his light raincoat as before, but with the pipe in his mouth. He realizes the fact before the guard does and puts the pipe back into his pocket.*)

I didn't feel like going home.

He sits down. / Display cases. Eighteenth- and nineteenth-century soldiers in uniform, 'Swiss men in foreign services', colourful, their gestures puppet-like, a drummer places his boot atop a drum, an officer ceremoniously holds up an old map, another looks through a long telescope and so on. Everything is motionless, viewed through the play of reflections on the glass. / A small boy in front of the glass case. / He suddenly sees, reflected in the glass, the seated raincoat-man rubbing his forehead.

BOY (*in Swiss dialect*).
    Daddy!

FATHER (*in Swiss dialect*).
    Come on, now.

BOY (*in Swiss dialect*).

  Daddy, one of them's still alive!

The bell rings. It's closing time.

Barbara at the end of her search, standing on a wooden quay. The lake is grey, the shore is invisible, an endless stretch of water, a few buoys here and there, no boats, seagulls on the buoys.

BARBARA.

  Teddy—

The boathouse—Yacht Club Turicum—is closed. An empty raft, the grey lake, the cries of the seagulls. / Ehrismann, in a bar at the central station. He sips an espresso, looking around furtively. There are no familiar faces here except for the Italian guest-worker who recognizes him. Ehrismann nods at him, which encourages the man to begin his lament once more.

GUEST-WORKER (*in Italian*).

  My fiancé—

EHRISMANN (*in Italian*).

  I understand.

GUEST-WORKER (*in Italian*).

  Dead.

Ehrismann doesn't turn away when the guest-worker pulls out the photograph from his pocket. He is grateful for some company.

EHRISMANN (*in Italian*).

>Would you like some coffee?

He orders one. / The bleached-out photograph in the worker's hand—a Calabrian family. Another photograph—a Calabrian girl.

GUEST-WORKER (*in Italian*).

>That's her. Look! My wife. You understand? Tomorrow is the funeral. Look! This one.
>
>(*Ehrismann looks at the photograph.*)
>
>I have no money to travel.
>
>(*The guest-worker begins to cry.*)
>
>I have no money—

Ehrismann returns the photograph.

EHRISMANN (*in Italian*).

>I understand.

GUEST WORKER (*in Italian*).

>It's true.

EHRISMANN (*in Italian*).

>How much is—

GUEST-WORKER (*in Italian*).

>The ticket?

EHRISMANN (*in Italian*).

>Yes.

GUEST-WORKER (*in Italian*).

>A lot, Sir, a lot. To Calabria! I don't know.

Ehrismann takes out his wallet—it is emptier than he imagined. He only finds a single bill, a fifty, which he offers to the man.

EHRISMANN (*in Italian*).
One moment.

GUEST-WORKER (*in Italian*).
Mamma mia, so much money! Fifty Swiss francs? Sir, you have saved the life of a poor immigrant. Saint Gennaro may protect you, you and your blessed family—

EHRISMANN (*in Italian*).
One moment.
(*He sees what else he's got—a British pound note and some coins. Not enough to get to Calabria. The young guest-worker, who was hoping to take off with the fifty, is startled when Ehrismann grabs his elbow.*)
Come!

GUEST-WORKER (*in Italian*).
Why?

EHRISMANN (*in Italian*).
Come!

He puts another coin down for the coffee.

GUEST WORKER (*in Italian*).
To the police?

EHRISMANN (*in Italian*).
To the bank.

They leave. / A bank counter. Marble. A cashier counts out bills, a customer waits. The process is a familiar one. It's all done very professionally. Only after all the money is handed over and then placed inside a briefcase does the cashier allows his face to soften into an expression of unofficial friendliness. The customer shakes his hand. The cashier then turns to the next man. A cheque needs to be processed. The cashier examines it, walks to the back, to a row of poeple at their computers, and asks a question. Something needs to be checked against the files. / Ehrismann at the counter, no longer quite the gentleman. Unshaved, his shirt is no longer fresh, the light raincoat slightly dirty. His sunglasses lend him a rather suspicious air. Hatless, his face is tense, nervous, insecure. / Finally, the cashier returns and calls out quietly—

CASHIER.

Herr Ehrismann?

(*Since nobody responds, he calls out a bit louder, bending closer to the counter—*)

Mister Ehrismann?

(*Ehrismann looks around to see if anyone in the hall is surprised at the name, but the hall is pretty empty. Only the young Italian sits among all the marble, / his hands between his knees, furtively glancing at his watch, a golden Omega. / Without saying a word, Ehrismann holds out his passport.*)

Herr Ehrismann—that's you?

(*Ehrismann nods. The passport seems to be fine. The cashier picks up a thick bundle of money.*)

My account was still alive.

While the money is being counted, at least fifteen thousand francs, a cry is heard—'La lizza delle Apuane', the call of the workers in the marble quarry of Carrara. / Then the song, 'Bella Ciao', sung by Italian guest-workers in a second-class compartment of the Swiss Federal train. / The hall at the central station. Ehrismann walks in with the young guest-worker, who is constantly trying to say goodbye to get him to leave. But Ehrismann has plenty of time. He accompanies the guest-worker to make sure he gets to the right platform, to the 'Gotthard–Chiasso–Milano' train. Ehrismann walks him to one of the compartments where a young woman waves through the open window and calls—

ITALIAN WOMAN (*in Italian*).

Hector! Hector!

Ehrismann recognizes her.

EHRISMANN (*in Italian*).

That's her, his fiancé—

He can't help but burst out laughing.

In the apartment, Monika's two brothers, still clad in their black coats, top hats in their hands. At a loss.

GOTTLIEB.

Monika?

(*There's no answer. In Swiss dialect—*)

I think we're ready to go now.

WILLY.

—Monika?

GOTTLIEB (*in Swiss dialect*).
    What's she doing?

Willy shrugs. / Monika, in the bedroom. Her veil lies black on the bed. Monika, in front of an open closet full of Ehrismann's shirts, ties, suits, shoes—very organized. She is no longer crying but deep in thought. We hear the brothers-in-law from the living room—

WILLY (*in Swiss dialect*).
    Monika, we're going now.

She doesn't respond.

GOTTLIEB (*in Swiss dialect*).
    Monika, we're going now.
    (*Monika ponders over what to do with the wardrobe of the deceased, then takes a suitcase from the closet, puts it on the floor and opens it. / The brothers, now wearing their top hats, appear in the door to say goodbye. / Monika lays piles of shirts in the suitcase. Gottlieb asks again, in Swiss dialect—*)
    Monika, what are you doing?

Monika doesn't respond but continues putting more shirts into the suitcase, then all of the ties. She is efficient and fast, seemingly unemotional but unstoppable. / The two brothers-in-law look at each other, unsure of what to make of the situation. / Monika then pulls out Ehrismann's trousers from the closet, pair after pair, and puts them in the suitcase, then jacket after jacket. Faster and faster. She cannot wait for the closet to be empty. Even when the suitcase is full, she cannot stop. Kneeling, she begins to throw out the shoes, her actions growing more and more out of control. We hear the music grow louder and louder, a music as strange as her behaviour, reckless-unhinged-otherworldly. Carnival music, / played by a group of grotesquely masked revellers, on trumpets and kettledrums. The carnival at night. A street in Zurich. The crowds in the mood for a last dance. A group of carnival-goers forms around the masked men and women, some people in costumes, some not. It is time for a midnight meal but the music excites the crowd. A masked woman starts to dance in the street, fearlessly. Alone at first. Then a man joins her, a 'Waggis' character with a rosy clown mask. The crowd in a circle around them begins to clap. The dance of the couple—half play, half orgy. The night-time facades of the old city resonate with carnival music, with grunting and quacking basses, with ambitious climbing clarinets mixed with the beat of the kettledrums that don't give a damn about the melody. A cacophony.

That's how we met.

When the music stops, the couple take off their masks. It is Monika and Ehrismann. Exhausted, they laugh and give each other a carnivalesque kiss that doesn't mean anything.

Our first kiss.

They separate, but the carnival music starts up again. Now everyone is marching, hand in hand, through the streets. Monika and Ehrismann, now unmasked, follow the music as it disappears into the narrow streets. / The two brothers-in-law, wearing their top hats.

WILLY.

Monika—

GOTTLIEB (*in Swiss dialect*).

We're going now.

(*Monika is no longer in the bedroom with the packed suit-case, the scattered shoes and her waiting brothers.*)

Monika!

(*He knocks on a door.*)

Monika, in front of the bathroom mirror. She places a necklace around her neck, stops, looks at herself in the mirror, then casually throws it into the toilet. It clinks softly. She does the same with her bracelet—she takes it off slowly, her face in the mirror revealing a certain contentment, then throws it into the toilet. Then she takes a small box and does the same with its contents which clink and clank—necklaces and rings and hairclips and brooches. For a moment she is startled. Then she pulls the flush.

Ehrismann, in his light raincoat, at a counter, waiting for his plane tickets.

STEWARD (*in English*).

Your luggage, Sir?

EHRISMANN (*in English*).

No luggage.

STEWARD (*in English*).

No luggage?

EHRISMANN (*in English*).
> No.

The steward points at the individual tickets.

STEWARD (*in English*).
> Zurich–Rome–Athens.
> (*Ehrismann nods. The steward continues in English—*)
> Athens–Cairo.
> (*Ehrismann nods. The steward continues in English—*)
> Cairo–Nairobi.

EHRISMANN.
> Okay.

STEWARD (*in English*).
> One way.
> (*He hands over the sleeve with the tickets. Then, in English*)
> You're welcome.
> (*Although he is done at the counter, Ehrismann remains, tickets in hand, as though waiting for something else. The steward says, in English—*)
> Eleven-fifty at the airport.

EHRISMANN (*in English*).
> Eleven-fifty—

I was surprised at how easy it was to leave Zurich behind.

EHRISMANN (*in English*).
> Thank you.

STEWARD (*in English*).
> You're welcome.

Ehrismann leaves, perplexed. / Again, the reckless-unhinged-otherworldly carnival music, the group of grotesque carnival figures with their trumpets and drums, everything as before only briefer. And when the masked couple take off their masks we see Monika and the young guest-worker, kissing.

Why should Monika not have another man?

Marching, hand in hand, through the streets / and, while the music grows quieter, Ehrismann, in his light raincoat, dancing on a banister at the Limmat river, / dancing atop a pole at a steamboat landing bridge, / dancing on the roof of the Bellevue kiosk during rush hour, / dancing at the edge of the roof of the Wasserkirche. / Ehrismann, in his light raincoat, at the railing of a tower of the Grossmünster—he waves his plane ticket at the town below, bathed in the light of the evening.

I was as free as never before!

While he waves, we hear the roar of a crowd. / A flood-lit ice hockey game in progress. The roar is of the spectators cheering their team. The attack is stopped in vain—the Czechs take over, the crowds are hushed, we can only hear the crash of the puck as it is passed from from stick to stick, fantastic, a fast and dangerous attack, the defence players slash the air, futile, now a shot at the goal but the puck smacks the post and the whole stadium exhales in relief. / The game, now on a TV screen watched by Barbara's husband, who also exhales in relief. He is standing, just come home from work. Then he takes off his jacket and sits in front of the TV. He is tense although not a lot is happening at the moment so he has time to light the forgotten cigarette between his lips. / Back to the stadium—another attack by the local team, the crowds cheer but the team is unlucky—players slip and fall. / The game, now on a different TV screen—a simple pub, some guests are watching, others not. In the foreground sits Viktor, his back to the TV, having a beer. / Back at the stadium—the crowds are hissing. / Again, on a TV screen—a pile of fallen players. / In the living room of a Zurichberg villa—the hissing won't stop, and, although it is muted, the mother-in-law is indignant.

MOTHER-IN-LAW (*in Swiss dialect*).

Is that necessary?

(*Willy turns a knob to lower the volume. The picture on the screen remains, though. The fallen players are getting to their feet, the referee has to intervene and issue a warning. A penalty is granted to one of the Czechs. / Back at the stadium—the bleachers, the spectators hissing at the Czech. / Again, on a TV screen—the crowds, their roaring muted. / Back at the stadium—Ehrismann, in his light raincoat, among some men who keep hissing. Ehrismann, the pipe in his mouth, looking amused / while the black-clad mother-in-law scolds once again, in Swiss dialect—*)

Willy—!

Willy reluctantly concedes that today is a day of mourning and gets up to turn off the TV. It is intermission now and the score is not encouraging: Czechoslovakia 3, Switzerland 1. Not a joyful day. What should the mourning family do? They sit waiting, as if life will not resume until tomorrow, / while the stadium resounds with a Vienna waltz blaring from the loudspeakers. Intermission. Seven men with shovels clean up the ice under the floodlights.

During intermission I thought again of Monika—

ANNOUNCER (*in Swiss dialect*).
Hot sausages!

A figure-skater enters the rink.

ANNOUNCER (*in Swiss dialect*).
Hot sausages!

She stands on her toes, raises her arms and takes position, then begins—first a pirouette, then a jump and so on. / The face of Monika as widow, the way Ehrismann saw her this morning at the crematorium. In the background, the waltz in the stadium

One year, and you'll be happy, Monika, half a year—

ANNOUNCER (*in Swiss dialect*).
Hot sausages!

Believe me.

ANNOUNCER (*in Swiss dialect*).
Hot sausages!

You wouldn't be the first woman who flourishes after losing her husband—

Applause in the stadium. / The figure-skater bows.

Believe me, Monika, believe me.

The figure-skater goes off the ice with a swing of her legs, casual yet graceful, and the two teams return, waving their sticks loosely by way of a warm up, until the referee whistles. The waltz breaks off.

ANNOUNCER (*in Swiss dialect*).

Hot sausages!

The puck drops, Face-off, the game continues, / Ehrismann amid the crowds, cheering with them. Focused on the game again, he stretches for a better view.

AUDIENCE.

Hopp Schwyz, Hopp Schwyz!

The sudden burst of confidence is quickly deflated and the 'Hopp' chorus falls silent. We hear the bang of the players hitting the boards. Ehrismann alone calls out—

EHRISMANN.

Hopp Schwyz!

I also thought of Barbara—

EHRISMANN.

Hopp Schwyz!

The surrounding spectators stare at him. / Barbara in a bubble bath, holding a whisky glass and laughing. / Back at the stadium—the Czechs are attacking again, and this time the puck doesn't hit the post but rolls into the net. Goal! / Continued on the TV screen—the Czechs hug their scorer, and Barbara's husband gets up to meet her at the door and take her coat. Barbara's face—tired, she seems to have realized that Ehrismann no longer exists. They sit down at the table. Her husband begins to pour wine into two glasses but stops when the crowds begin to roar and turns off the TV. / At the stadium—the Czech goalie, lying on the ice, gets up listlessly and takes the black puck out of the net. The Swiss hug their scorer, / and Ehrismann stands silent among the cheering crowds.

Still a long time until midnight.

Ehrismann on a park bench.

So that would be my last evening in Zurich—

He gets up. / The searchlight of the control tower at Kloten Airport, engine noises from afar, a jet scream slowly fades. / Viktor in his atelier.

The only person to whom I could have gone was Viktor.

Viktor in his pajamas. A Chianti bottle in hand, he walks over to his work table to look for a glass. He finds one—it is dirty, and he needs to rinse it under a tap.

VIKTOR.
Nairobi?
(*Then he fills the glass.*)
I think it's great.
(*He looks for a second glass. We can see a painting on an easel, tools, paintings leaning against the walls, frames, a metal sculpture. Not a romantic atelier but a workshop.*)
Feel free to look around.
(*He finds a second glass—this too is dirty, and needs to be rinsed clean.*)

When does your plane leave?

(*He laughs.*)

Do you remember? You were the one who told me back then?—'Don't allow yourself to be defeated, give it up and do what you're tempted to do!'

And he did.

Viktor fills a second glass.

VIKTOR.

Why did you never show up again?

(*He puts away the Chianti bottle, takes the two full glasses and steps forward so that only his face is visible. No longer young but not exhausted either. His voice is dry but warm.*)

Honestly, I think it's the right thing to do!

(*Then he holds out one of the two glasses, / while Ehrismann, in his light raincoat, walks through the hall at the airport.*)

Cheers!

Neon brightness. Everything is deserted. The kiosk is closed. Outside in the night, two jets gleam in the glow of the floodlights. Ehrismann, alone in the airport hall. The coffee bar is closed too but, through the glass door, we can see a waitress cleaning up at the buffet, and two cleaning ladies lifting up chairs and placing them on the tables, upside down. A dull room. / Ehrismann, at the glass door. He knocks / and the waitress looks up—she is annoyed at first and then her expression changes.

I didn't expect that—

She comes to open the door.

WAITRESS.

Ehrismann—

EHRISMANN.

Yes.

WAITRESS (*in French*).

How are you doing?

(*She seems happy to see an old friend again, while Ehris-mann, not recognized and not spoken to since his funeral, smiles like someone who's been caught. And, since there is nothing to confess to, he remains silent.*)

How are you doing?

(*She takes him into the bar.*)

EHRISMANN (*in French*).

—I'm okay.

He stands there, a little lost and uncomprehending. He sees the chairs on the tables, sees the cleaning ladies, and then realizes that the bar is closed. His confusion is visible but he doesn't understand that *she* isn't confused.

WAITRESS (*in French*).

I'm Yvette!

She laughs.

EHRISMANN (*in French*).

How are you?

(*He doesn't expect an answer. The sound of an engine fil-ters in, muted, through the glass walls—a persistent nasty monotone, not loud but irritating.*)

Do you have anything left to drink?

YVETTE (*in French*).
What would you like?

EHRISMANN.
Coffee.

(*He reads her expression—no more coffee.*)

Or kirsch schnapps.

(*She takes a bottle from the bar while he looks her over—
an old acquaintance, no beauty, by the way, perhaps even
a little spent, but blissfully chipper, slightly witch-like, with
a tendency to giggle regardless of the situation. She speaks
German with a West Swiss accent—delicate—and she
always sounds a bit like she is joking. This makes it hard
to ask a serious question.*)

Tell me—

She fills a small glass, tired, but happy to see Ehrismann
again. She asks, in confidence and without affectation—

YVETTE.
What are you doing?

EHRISMANN.
I live.

She giggles.

YVETTE.
You live!

EHRISMANN.
Yes.

(*It doesn't seem to surprise her at all.*)

And what are you doing?

YVETTE.

I work.

He has sat down, drained, on the only chair that the cleaning ladies haven't put away. Yet his posture and expression suggest he is alert, on the look-out, as if hunted by the police, uneasy. She hands him the kirsch schnapps.

EHRISMANN.

Tell me—

YVETTE.

What's the matter with you?

EHRISMANN.

Why?

(*She giggles.*)

Tell the truth—don't you know or are you pretending?

(*An incomprehensible announcement rumbles through the loudspeaker. Ehrismann listens, then downs the kirsch.*)

You don't read the newspapers?

YVETTE (*in French*).

Why?

(*He drinks again from his empty glass and stays silent as one of the cleaning ladies passes, by looking sullen.*)

We're leaving, yes, we're leaving!

(*Yvette makes a face at her retreating back, then she points out to Ehrismann, who is still holding his glass—*)

We're closing.

(*She pulls off her waitress' apron.*)

EHRISMANN.

You haven't heard of my accident?

YVETTE.

Accident?

EHRISMANN.

You didn't read about it?

YVETTE.

What accident?

EHRISMANN.

A tragic accident.

YVETTE.

Seriously?

EHRISMANN.

I am dead.

(*She giggles.* / *Outside in the night, the jet planes gleam beneath the floodlights, the fuel truck is leaving, a crowd of passengers walks to the plane to board his flight.* / *Ehrismann, sitting as before.*)

You don't believe me?

YVETTE.

That you're dead?

EHRISMANN.

Seriously.

For her, the joke is over.

YVETTE (*in French*).

I'm tired.

EHRISMANN (*in French*).

Me too.

(*She disappears behind the buffet. Again, an incomprehensible announcement. Ehrismann doesn't listen.*)

I haven't slept even an hour. Yesterday, in London. And this morning, when I wanted to sleep on the plane—the obituary notice.

YVETTE (*in French*).

What are you saying?

EHRISMANN.

My obituary.

(*Yvette comes back.*)

And then this whole funeral!

Yvette, who has fetched her coat and is putting it on, stops, unsure for a moment what he means by that joke—

YVETTE.

Which funeral?

EHRISMANN.

Protestant.

(*He gets up and puts the empty glass on the counter, puts the pipe in his mouth, while Yvette is looking for her head-cloth. He wants to light his pipe but there is no more tobacco in it.*)

Cremation.

He knocks the ash out of the pipe. / Outside in the deserted airport hall—the crackle of the loudspeaker interrupts the silence as yet another announcement is about to begin, and then a female voice speaking very clearly—

LOUDSPEAKER (*in English*).

Mister Ehrismann, Passenger to Rome–Athens– Cairo, Mister Ehrismann—

(*The loudspeaker crackles again. / Yvette, now wearing her head-cloth, locks up the buffet. The loudspeaker again, in English—*)

This is our last call.

The loudspeaker crackles and is silent.

YVETTE.

You have to go!

A cleaning lady picks up the chair behind Ehrismann and places it upside down on one of the tables.

EHRISMANN.

What am I supposed to do in Nairobi?

(*He stands there, aimless.*)

They buried me. Peace be with me. I was there. You don't believe me?

(*He picks up the phone beside the cash counter.*)

Then call my widow—

YVETTE.

(*Beginning in French—*) You're crazy!

(*He dials the number.*)

You'll be late.

He waits for the dial tone.

EHRISMANN.

Here—

(*He hands her the receiver.*)

Tell her I'm alive. Monika, that's her name. Tell her we went to school together and that I'm standing beside you.

(*She hesitantly holds the receiver to her ear.*)

But say it kindly.

She abruptly puts the receiver down.

YVETTE (*in French*).

You really are crazy!

She thinks she's being fooled. / Outside in the night, the engines of the jet have been turned on, the gangway has been removed, the doors closed, a man in a white jumpsuit gives the signal and, slowly, the plane rolls on. The whistling of the jet nozzles. / Ehrismann, the phone receiver in his hand, has dialed the number again and is pretending that this is just a joke, but he hesitates—his jesting expression fades.

EHRISMANN.

Hello?

YVETTE (*in French*).

Are you really married?

EHRISMANN.

Hello!

The noise of the jet engine is deafening. / Night in the Ehrismann apartment. Silence. The beautiful cat is sleeping in her basket. The light from a streetlamp. We hear the phone ring, then stop. / Night at the airport. The lights along the runway, the roar of the jet taking off, we can only see its running lights which, immediately after take-off, go dark. All that remains are the blinking lights of the steeply rising plane.

Ehrismann in the hallway where he has turned on the light. Ehrismann in his light raincoat that he won't take off. Standing, as he had been in the National Museum, hands in his pockets. Someone who looks but does not touch. / The living room in full view, lit only by the light from the hallway. Silence. / Close-up of the glass table with the seven cups left by the mourning family. Flowers, many flowers, everywhere. / A black top hat on the record player. / More flowers. / On a trunk lies a heap of condolence letters and black-edged cards. Ehrismann does not touch them, just reads the one on top and then slowly moves on. / The lit hallway without Ehrismann. We hear his footsteps, then silence, then his footsteps again. / Close-up of Ehrismann. Indifferent, alert but uninvolved. / The door to a room. Ehrismann knocks softly, waits, knocks again, listens, opens the door and turns on the light. The master bedroom. The open suitcase with his shirts and ties, the shoes on the floor, the open closet, the black widow's veil on the bed. / His mother-in-law is sitting beside a bed. The wallpaper of a child's room. By the glow of a bedside lamp we see the peaceful face of the sleeping widow, her bare shoulder, her hair loose on the pillow.

Nobody was home.

His mother-in-law carefully pulls the blanket over Monika's bare shoulder, not wanting to wake her, and says quietly—

MOTHER-IN-LAW (*in Swiss dialect*).
It's nice, child, that you're back.

She turns off the bedside lamp / while Ehrismann now turns on the lights everywhere else in the apartment. The light in the kitchen. Flowers here too. He takes a glass, fills it with water, drinks, fills it a second time and drinks. He sees the cat sleeping in her basket.

EHRISMANN.
Bimbo?
(*The cat sleeps on. / The lights in the living room. The ceiling light, the table lamp, the floor lamp, as much light as possible, another floor lamp, then Ehrismann sees himself in a large mirror. He smiles at his reflection, then moves on. / The blank mirror. We can hear his footsteps, silence, then a sudden quiet clank. / Ehrismann, beside the glass table—his coat has knocked over a cup. He puts it back and dries the table carefully with his handkerchief. / The cat at the door to the living room.*)
Bimbo!
(*He throws the cat a biscuit from the funeral leftovers on the table. It sniffs the offering, then turns away. / Ehrismann takes a second biscuit to throw to the cat, and a third, then gives up.*)

The light is on in the studio. His desk with its drawers open—it has been searched for documents. Papers strewn all over. / Ehrismann looks at but does not touch—close-up—an insurance policy, / a dried starfish, / a notebook in grey linen, 'Work Book', a label with name–year of birth–place of residence–service rank, / all sorts of keys, / headache pills, / a diploma certificate from the Swiss Federal Institute of Technology, / a flashlight, / neat stacks of cheque receipts, / a bronze medal, / a folder labelled 'Swiss Credit Institute', / seashells, / a thick bundle of yellowing letters with a handwritten note 'Private', tied up and sealed with a knot, / a photo of him as a child wearing a sailor's collar. / Ehrismann in his light raincoat, hands in his pockets, the cold pipe in his mouth. Standing. Unaffected. / His face, suddenly breaking into joy. / Many pipes in a pipe holder. He picks up one of them, a Dunhill Number 4, then puts another back, the Parker he has had in his mouth all day, making sure that the arrangement in the holder looks unchanged. / His face with the Dunhill pipe. Content. / Studio, living room, hallway—everywhere, the lights are switched off. Darkness. We hear the front door close. / Ehrismann in the stairwell, lighting his pipe before walking down the stairs. Suddenly, we hear footsteps coming up. Ehrismann holds his breath. No smoking, then. The steps come closer and closer, then we hear the door of the apartment on the floor below. He waits. Voices from downstairs, then silence. He peers down, then tiptoes forward. Downstairs, where the mailboxes are, he opens the front door, holds it open with his foot and then throws his keys into the mailbox where they fall with a clatter. / The keys in the mailbox. / Ehrismann, outside on the dark street. He walks on as if nothing has happened, then stops a little later to light his pipe. Someone passes by. Ehrismann greets him and walks on, / while the passer-by, the old man who had expressed his sympathies in the morning, cannot believe his eyes and turns around./ The street is dark. And empty.

APPENDIX I

ORIGINAL DIALOGUES IN ITALIAN / FRENCH

PAGE 23

WAITER.
Dove soni i panini?

PAGE 24

WAITRESS.
Panini!

WAITER.
Panini!

GUEST WORKER.
Morta! Morta! Mia Moglie. Capisce? Morta. Ed io: senza soldi. Capisce? Senza franchi—

[. . .]

Eccola. Guardi! La mia fidanzata. Morta. Questa. Morta. Domani c'è il funerale. Guardi! Questa—

[. . .]

Gli Svizzeri non capiscono mai!

[. . .]

PAGE 25

WAITER.
Basta! *Allora basta*!

PAGE 26

WAITER.
Allora Basta!

PAGE 47

EHRISMANN.
Come va?

MAID.
Signore—

EHRISMANN.
Va bene?

MAID.
O Dio—

EHRISMANN.
Un miracolo, eh?
[. . .]

PAGE 53

GUEST-WORKER.
La mia fidanzata—

EHRISMANN.
Ho capito.

GUEST-WORKER.
Morta.

Page 54

EHRISMANN.

Prende un caffè?

[. . .]

GUEST-WORKER.

Eccola. Guardi! Mia moglie. Capisce? Domani c'è il funerale. Guardi! Questa.

[. . .]

Non ho soldi per viaggiare.

[. . .]

Non ho soldi—

[. . .]

EHRISMANN.

Ho capito.

GUEST WORKER.

E vero.

EHRISMANN.

Quanto costa—

GUEST-WORKER.

Il biglietto?

EHRISMANN.

Si.

GUEST-WORKER.

Molto, Signore, molto. Per Calabria! Non lo so.

Page 55

EHRISMANN.
Momento.

GUEST-WORKER.
Mamma mia, quanti soldi! Cinquanta franchi svizzeri?
Signore, Lei ha salvato un povero emigrato. Che San Gen-
naro Lei protegga, Lei e la sua benedetta famiglia—

EHRISMANN.
Momento.
[. . .]
Venga!

GUEST-WORKER.
Perchè?

EHRISMANN.
Venga!

[. . .]

GUEST WORKER.
Alla polizia?

EHRISMANN.
Alla banca.

PAGE 57

ITALIAN WOMAN.
Ettore! Ettore!

[. . .]

EHRISMANN.
Ecco, la sua fidanzata—

PAGE 68

WAITRESS.

Comment ça va?

[. . .]

Comment ça va?

[. . .]

EHRISMANN.

—*ça va, ça va.*

WAITRESS.

Je suis Yvette!

[. . .]

EHRISMANN.

Comment ça va?

[. . .]

PAGE 69

YVETTE.

Qu'est-ce que tu veux?

PAGE 70

YVETTE.

Pourquoi?

[. . .]

On s'en va, oui, on s'en va!

[. . .]

On ferme.

[. . .]

PAGE 71

YVETTE.
Je suis fatiguée.

PAGE 72

EHRISMANN.
Moi aussi.
[. . .]
YVETTE.
Qu'est-ce que tu dis?

PAGE 73

YVETTE.
Tu es fou!
[. . .]

PAGE 74

YVETTE.
Mais tu es vraiment fou!

YVETTE.
Tu es vraiment marié?

APPENDIX 2

ENGLISH TRANSLATIONS OF FRENCH SONG LYRICS

PAGE 27

JUKEBOX.

> 'No, not one single thing
> No, I don't regret a thing
> Not the good come my way
> Nor the ill
> It's all equal to me', etc.

JUKEBOX.

> 'Oh my memories
> Have lit a fire
> My pains, my pleasures
> I can now do without', etc.

PAGE 28

JUKEBOX.

> 'No, not one single thing
> No, I don't regret a thing', etc.

PAGE 29

JUKEBOX.

> 'Come here, My Lord!'

[. . .]

JUKEBOX.

'Come here, My Lord!'

[. . .]

JUKEBOX.

'Come here, My Lord!'

PAGE 30

JUKEBOX.

'What, are you crying, My Lord? That, I would never have thought.'

[. . .]

JUKEBOX.

'Yes, dance, My Lord!'